Full

Understanding

1

by Denise Justice-France

ISBN-13: 978-1530401840

ISBN-10: 1530401844

To get full understanding of the word, you must read the the complete scriptures and not just one scripture; because the scriptures will explain the meaning of each verse by reading the complete scriptures, which is a verse before and after a verse.

The LORD brought this is to my attention when I heard so many verses quoted, and it is spoken about that particular verse alone. The other verses were not quoted.

These are verse that I have heard time and time again.

But with different meaning:

For instance:

You think about prosperity?

"Be not deceived; God is not mocked: for whatsoever a man soweth, that shall he shall reap."

Galatians 6:7

But what about the next verse.

"For he that soweth to his flesh shall of the flesh reap corruption;but he that soweth to the Spirit shall of the Spirit reap life everlasting.

Galatians 6:8

It is about your flesh and everlasting life.

About Asking?

"and all things, whatsoever ye shall ask in prayer, believing, ye shall receive."
  Matthew 21:22

But the verse before this

Jesus answered and said unto them, Verily   I say unto you, If ye have faith, and doubt not, ye shall not only do this which is done to the fig tree, but also if ye shall say unto this mountain, Be thou removed and be thou cast into the sea; it shall be done.

Matthew 21:21
It is about your faith in God.

About giving and receiving?

"but this I say, He which soweth sparingly shall reap also sparingly; and he which soweth bountifully shall reap also bountifully.

2 Corinthians 9:6

But the verse after is:

"Every man according as he purposeth in his heart, so let him give; not grudgingly, or of necessity: for God loveth a cheerful giver.

2 Corinthians 9:7

One verse further

"and God is able to make all grace abound toward you; that ye, always having all sufficiency in all things, may abound to every good work:(As it is written, He hath dispersed abroad; he hath given to the poor; his righteousness remainth forever.

2 Corinthians 9:8

One more further verse

"Now he that ministered seed to the soweth both minister bread for your food, and multiply your seed sown, and increase the fruits of your righteousness;)

2 Corinthians 9:10

This is talking about God you has given us his Son to let us know that he loves us so much. He gave us his son which was the word and the word became flesh in his Son for us. He gave us cheerfully and happy to deliver us from this world for everlasting life.

The following verse explains this:

Thanks be to God for His indescribable gift!

2 Corinthians 9:15

<u>I thought it was about speaking things to make it to come to pass?</u>

"For verily I say unto you, That whosoever shall say unto this mountain, Be thou removed, and be thou cast into the sea; and shall not doubt in his heart, but shall believe that those things which he saith shall come to pass; he shall have whatsoever he saith;

MARK 11:23

But the verse before

"and Peter called to remembrance saith unto him, Master, behold, the fig tree which thou cursedst is withered away."

Mark 11:21

"and Jesus answered saith unto them, Have faith in God.   Mark 11:22

This is talking about faith in God.

<u>I thought it was about desires?</u>

"Therefore I say unto you, What things soever ye desire, when ye pray, believe that ye receive them, and ye shall have them.

Mark 11:24

But the verse after is:

"And when ye stand praying, forgive, if ye have ought against any: that your Father also which is in heaven may forgive you your trespasses.

Mark 11:25

This is talking about forgiveness because God forgave us all for our lustful desires that was not his will.

But if ye do not forgive, neither will your Father which is in heaven forgive your trespasses.

Mark 11:26

I thought it was about money?

"And the Lord shall make thee the head, and not the tail; and thou shall be above only, and thou shall not beneath; if that thou hearken unto the commandments of the Lord thy God, which I command thee this day, to observe and to them.

Deuteronomy 28:13

But the verse before:

"The Lord shall make thee plenteous in goods, in the fruit of thy body, and in the fruit of thy cattle, and in the fruit of thy ground, in the land which the Lord sware unto thy fathers to give thee.

And the Lord shall open unto thee his good treasure, the heaven to give the rain unto thy land in his season, and to bless all the work of thine hand: and thou shalt lend unto many nations, and thou shall not borrow.

Deuteronomy 28:11-12

This is talking about the Lord will provide for me.

"and thou shall not go aside from any of the words which I command thee this day, to the right hand, or to the left, to go after other gods to serve them.

Deuteronomy 28:14

Heard about saying and it will come to you, if you have faith in it?

"Now faith is the substance of things hoped for, the evidence of things not seen."

Hebrews 11:3

But it is about faith in God.

The whole chapter of Hebrews tell us this.
Faith in God

About evil?

"No weapon what is formed against thee shall prosper"

Isaiah 54:17

But the completed verse is

"No weapon that is formed against thee shall prosper; and every tongue that shall rise against thee in judgment thou shalt condemn. This is the heritage of the servants of the Lord, and their righteousness is of me, saith the Lord. "

Isaiah 54:17

But a couple of verses before this:

And all thy children shall be taught of the Lord; and great be the peace of thy children.

Isaiah 54:13

In righteousness shalt thou be established: thou shall be far from oppression; for thou shalt not fear: and from terror, for it shall not come near thee.

Isaiah 54:14

"Behold, I have created the smith that bloweth the coals in the fire, and that bringeth forth an instrument for his work; and I have created the waster to destroy.

Isaiah 54:15

This is about evil and the evil remove from us because we believe in him.

"Fear not; for thou shall not be ashamed: neither be thou confounded; for thou shalt not be put to shame: for thou shalt forget the shame of thy youth, and shalt not remember the reproach of thy widowhood any more.

Isaiah 54:4

<u>Because</u>

"For thy Maker is thine husband; the LORD OF Hosts is his name; and thy Redeemer the Holy One of Israel; The God of the whole earth shall be called.

Isaiah 54:5

<u>and that's WHY?</u>

"No weapon that is formed against the shall prosper; and every tongue that shall rise against thee in judgment thou shalt condemn. This is the heritage of the servants of the Lord, and their righteousness is of me, saith the Lord.

Isaiah 54:17

See about evil

Isaiah 54:17 is the last verse in this chapter that explains it all thought out the chapter.

About Worry?

"Therefore, I say unto you, Take no thought for your life, what ye shall eat, or what ye shall drink; nor yet for your body, what ye shall put on. Is not he life more than meat, and the body than raiment?

Matthew 6:25

The verse before this is:

"No one can serve two masters; for either he will hate one, and love the other; or else he will hold to the one, and despite the other. Ye cannot serve God and mammon.

Matthew 6:24

The verse after is:

"Behold the fowls of the air; for they sown not, neither do they reap, nor gather into barns; yet your heavenly Father feedeth them. Are ye not much better than they?

Matthew 6:26

God is saying do not serve money to get more and more and worrying about how to get more because he provides for us then he show us an example.

Example

"take heed that ye do not your alms before men, to be seen of them: otherwise ye have no reward of your Father which is in heaven.

Matthew 6:1

Verse after:

"therefore when thou doest thine alms, do not sound a trumpet before thee, as the hypocrites do in the synagogues and in the streets., that they may have glory of men. Verily i say unto you, they have their reward.

Matthew 6:2

Again

"Behold the fowls of the air; for they sow not neither do they reap, nor gather into barns; ye your heavenly Father feedeth them. Are you not much better than they?

Matthew 6:26

which of you by taking thought can add one cubit unto his stature?   Matthew   6:27

And why take ye though for raiment? Consider the lilies of the field, how they grow; they toil not, neither do they spin:

Matthew 6:28

and yet I say unto you, that even Solomon in all his glory was not arrayed like one of these.

Matthew 6:29

"Wherefore, if God so clothe the grass of the field, which to day is, and to morrow is cast into the oven, shall he not much more clothe you. O ye of little faith?

Matthews 6:30

"therefore take no thought, saying, What shall we eat? or, What shall we drink? or, Wherewithal shall we be clotherd?   (For all these things do the

Gentiles seek:) for your heavenly Father knoweth that ye have need of all these things. But seek ye first the Kingdom of God, and his righteousness, ad all these things shall be added unto you.

Matthew 6:31-33

I do not know why the Lord instructed me to write these things because I do not know all and I am not by no means a perfect person, but I believe that the Lord was helping me with problems that I was having in my life with different scriptures.

Because I have heard so many scriptures and so many times I did not understand what I was hearing.

So the Lord instructed me to look deeper into this word and to get true understanding and meaning of his word.

So I will continue to do his will for my Life and continue to read the bible thoroughly and pray for understanding and wisdom.

this is my interpretation of these things and my thoughts and no one else.

Acknowledgment:

Thank you father for helping me to understand your word and continue to work with me Lord.

Because I am sinner and I repent.
Give me Full Understanding

www.ingramcontent.com/pod-product-compliance
Lightning Source LLC
Chambersburg PA
CBHW060820290526
45792CB00005BB/1736